SCENES FROM
FAMILY LIFE

by Mark Ravenhill

SAMUEL FRENCH

samuelfrench.co.uk

THINKING ABOUT PERFORMING A SHOW?

There are thousands of plays and musicals available to perform from Samuel French right now, and applying for a licence is easier and more affordable than you might think

---

From classic plays to brand new musicals, from monologues to epic dramas, there are shows for everyone.

Plays and musicals are protected by copyright law, so if you want to perform them, the first thing you'll need is a licence. This simple process helps support the playwright by ensuring they get paid for their work and means that you'll have the documents you need to stage the show in public.

Not all our shows are available to perform all the time, so it's important to check and apply for a licence before you start rehearsals or commit to doing the show.

LEARN MORE & FIND THOUSANDS OF SHOWS

Browse our full range of plays and musicals, and find out more about how to license a show

www.samuelfrench.co.uk/perform

Talk to the friendly experts in our Licensing team for advice on choosing a show and help with licensing

plays@samuelfrench.co.uk   020 7387 9373

Acting Editions

BORN TO PERFORM

Playscripts designed from the ground up to work the way you do in rehearsal, performance and study

---

Larger, clearer text for easier reading

Wider margins for notes

Performance features such as character and props lists, sound and lighting cues, and more

---

+ CHOOSE A SIZE AND STYLE TO SUIT YOU

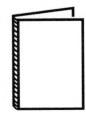

STANDARD EDITION

Our regular paperback book at our regular size

SPIRAL-BOUND EDITION

The same size as the Standard Edition, but with a sturdy, easy-to-fold, easy-to-hold spiral-bound spine

LARGE EDITION

A4 size and spiral bound, with larger text and a blank page for notes opposite every page of text – perfect for technical and directing use

LEARN MORE | samuelfrench.co.uk/actingeditions

**Other plays by MARK RAVENHILL
published by Samuel French**

Candide

Citizenship

Ghost Story

Golden Child

Handbag

Mother Clap's Molly House

Over There

Pool (No Water)

Product

Shoot/Get Treasure/Repeat

Shopping and Fucking

Some Explicit Polaroids

The Cut

The Experiment

**FIND PERFECT PLAYS TO PERFORM AT
www.samuelfrench.co.uk/perform**

ABOUT THE AUTHOR

Mark Ravenhill was born in Haywards Heath, West Sussex in 1966. He studied Drama and English at Bristol University. His first play *Shopping and Fucking* was produced by Out of Joint and the Royal Court Theatre in 1996. Subsequent plays include *Faust Is Dead* and *Handbag* (both Actors Touring Company), *Some Explicit Polaroids* (Out of Joint at the Ambassadors Theatre), *Mother Clap's Molly House* and *Citizenship* (both National Theatre), *Pool (No Water)* (Frantic Assembly at the Lyric Theatre), *The Cut* (Donmar Theatre), *Shoot/Get Treasure/Repeat* (Paines Plough) and *Over There* (Royal Court). From 2012 to 2014, Mark was playwright in residence for the Royal Shakespeare Company, producing a new version of Brecht's *Galileo* and a new play *Candide* inspired by Voltaire (both Swan Theatre, Stratford-Upon-Avon). Mark's work in music theatre includes a new English version of Monteverdi's *The Coronation of Poppea* with additional material by Michael Nyman (King's Head); *Ten Plagues*, a song cycle for Marc Almond with composer Connor Mitchell (Traverse Theatre) and *Elysium* with composer Rolf Wallin for the Norwegian Opera. Mark is the co-creator of the ITV sitcom *Vicious*.

MUSIC USE NOTE

Licensees are solely responsible for obtaining formal written permission from copyright owners to use copyrighted music in the performance of this play and are strongly cautioned to do so. If no such permission is obtained by the licensee, then the licensee must use only original music that the licensee owns and controls. Licensees are solely responsible and liable for all music clearances and shall indemnify the copyright owners of the play(s) and their licensing agent, Samuel French, against any costs, expenses, losses and liabilities arising from the use of music by licensees. Please contact the appropriate music licensing authority in your territory for the rights to any incidental music.

IMPORTANT BILLING AND CREDIT REQUIREMENTS

If you have obtained performance rights to this title, please refer to your licensing agreement for important billing and credit requirements.

Scenes from Family Life was commissioned as part of the National Theatre Connections programme and first presented in July 2008.

CHARACTERS

JACK

LISA

STACY

BARRY

A GROUP OF THEIR FRIENDS

THREE SOLDIERS

PARENTS AND BABIES GROUP

MOTHER WITH AN EMPTY PRAM

ENTERTAINER

All characters are aged sixteen to eighteen

SETTING

Living room of Jack and Lisa's flat

Scene One

Living room of JACK *and* LISA's *flat.*

LISA Feel?

JACK Yeah.

JACK *reaches out and touches* LISA's *stomach.*

LISA Head and feet and... Tiny but somewhere there's...

JACK Yeah.

LISA You thought of names?

JACK Not yet. You?

LISA A few but... Don't want to jinx it.

JACK Too soon.

LISA Yeah.

JACK What's it feel like?

LISA Different.

JACK Does it send you messages and stuff? Through your body?

LISA I dunno. Maybe. Yeah.

JACK You gotta know.

LISA No.

JACK What's going on in your head?

LISA Happiness. You. Me. Baby.

JACK That all?

LISA Yeah.

JACK You sure...?

LISA I can't tell you every—

JACK But that's what I want to know.

LISA It's just not possible. You ready to be a dad?

JACK I am totally, totally ready.

LISA My mum, she says we're too young but I say Jack's got a job, I got a job, we got the flat, it's time. I love you.

JACK And I love you.

They kiss.

Together forever. You feel trapped?

LISA No. Love it. Love you.

JACK Am I boring?

LISA Normal.

JACK I'll get the tea.

Exit JACK. *Whoosh, flash,* LISA *vanishes into thin air. Re-enter* JACK.

Lisa, do you want white or the...? Lees? Lees? Lisa?

Pause.

Lisa?

Pause.

Lisa!

Pause.

Lisa?

He hunts around the room.

I'm gonna find you and when I find you I'm gonna... Lisa?

He goes and checks in the bedroom.

(offstage) Lisa!

He enters from the bedroom. She reappears – a rematerialisation.

Oh my god. Oh my oh oh—

LISA What? What?

JACK I... There was nothing there. It was frightening. There was like this gap where a person should be and I was calling out but there was nothing there. And then you were there.

LISA Stop messing around.

JACK I'm not, I – Oh Lees. You think I'm going mad? Maybe...

LISA Forget it. Trick of the light. Kiss me.

JACK Listen I...can't.

LISA You're scared of me.

JACK No just I—

LISA You are. You're scared of me.

JACK Of course if you can just—

LISA I'm solid – I'm real – you see – you see – touch me – touch me – what do you feel?

JACK Yeah solid, real yeah.

LISA So I'm here. Nothing happened. You're very tired. You're very stressed. Nobody's running away. Nobody's fading. I'm here with you. We're gonna have the baby together. We're gonna be together – forever. Yeah?

JACK Yeah. Yeah. Yeah.

LISA Daddy.

JACK Mummy.

LISA You feeling alright now?

JACK Yeah.

Whooshing sounds. Flashing lights. She's vanished.

Oh no oh no oh no oh – hello hello hello – oh no please!
Are you there? Are you – oh oh oh oh. Oh please don't do
this oh please oh – I don't want to be on my own. I don't
like being on my own. Oh oh oh.

Flashing and whooshing. Blackout. Full light. **LISA** *is
back.*

LISA Can I do the curry now?

JACK You did it again. You vanished. Faded away and then—

LISA You're mad.

JACK Stop doing it.

LISA This is completely mad.

JACK I want you to stop doing that. I don't like it.

LISA I'm not doing anything. I'm living with a freak.

JACK There's a place up there or down there or in there or...
somewhere and you are going there.

LISA I have had enough of this. I've wanted this baby ever since
I was thirteen and now you, you – I'm going out.

JACK Where?

LISA I don't know. Shops. Cinema. Mates. Anywhere.

JACK But what if you vanish—? In front of your mates?

LISA Not gonna happen. Good night.

JACK Stay here.

LISA Why?

JACK It'll be safer.

LISA You're making me frightened.

JACK With the current circumstances.

LISA There are no...

JACK I'll look after you. Stay. Stay. Stay in the house. How we gonna look after baby if you don't stay in the house?

LISA How can we if you keep—?

JACK It's not me it's you who's vanishing.

LISA See. See. We're incompatible.

JACK No no I do love you Lees I do, I just – something's going on – I don't understand but there is something but I – oh – but I do want the baby so...

LISA Alright but – listen – you gotta cut out the funny stuff. I want normal. That's important.

JACK I'll try to cut out the—

LISA Normal. Yeah – I just can't handle. There's a world out there of people and they're all odd. They seem odd. They have like freak-outs on buses and stuff. Talk to themselves. Punch strangers. I can't handle that. You're normal. That's why I picked you.

JACK Course.

LISA I gotta have a totally normal baby father.

JACK I'm the one. Maybe I'm...tonight means so much I'm just...didn't think I was nervous but maybe I'm...

LISA Come here.

JACK Yeah.

Whooshing, flashing etc. JACK *rapidly gets out his mobile phone. Starts video recording.* LISA *vanishes.*

Come on come on.

Whooshing flashing etc, LISA *reappears.*

You did it again.

LISA No I never I was just—

JACK You did. Look.

> JACK *rewinds the images, indicates to* LISA *to have a look on the phone.*

LISA This is stupid I'm not gonna just—

> *Reluctantly, she looks.*

...Oh my god. Thin air and then I... That's so frightening. Hold me. Oh babe.

JACK *(holds her)* I know, I know.

LISA Am I solid now? I feel solid.

JACK You are. You're solid now.

LISA What we gonna do? If I'm the kind of person who just vanishes – I don't wanna be the kind of person who just vanishes. I never heard of that...people who just...oh.

JACK Me neither.

LISA I want to be here forever.

> *Doorbell.*

JACK I'll do it.

> JACK *answers it. Enter* BARRY *and* STACY, *who is eight months pregnant.*

BARRY Will you tell her, will you tell her—?

STACY Just watch him.

BARRY Will you two tell her—? Will you tell her – she's got this idea, she's got this really stupid idea—

STACY It's not—

BARRY She says that I'm vanishing. She says—

STACY He has.

BARRY I haven't.

STACY You have. You fade in front of my eyes – you go to nothing.

BARRY Will one of you, both of you, tell her that she is mad? Hormones.

STACY I'm not—

BARRY People don't just vanish. I try but I – it's the baby playing with her hormones, she doesn't – when women are pregnant they get these... Your head gets muddled up. You cry and then you're happy and then I vanish.

JACK Barry, mate—

BARRY Yeah? *(to* STACY*)* Listen to this—

JACK Barry, mate, it's true. People vanish. Lisa's doing the same. Today I've seen—

BARRY Jesus.

JACK Three times. People vanish. I never thought 'til today. But I've seen it. You can just...lose people. They fade to nothing. Empty.

Beat.

BARRY *(to* STACY*)* You set him up to this.

STACY I didn't do nothing.

BARRY Lisa?

LISA It's true. I'm not a solid person. I'm a person who just... goes and comes back again.

BARRY You're all mad. What you been doing? Well, I'm not going to vanish. Why am I gonna vanish? I'm not gonna vanish. Not gonna vanish when I got a kid on the way.

LISA Show him the clip.

JACK Look at this. *(He shows* BARRY *and* STACY *the phone clip.)*

LISA See? I go to nothing.

BARRY ...Oh my god... Is that what I...?

STACY Just the same. Same as you.

BARRY Oh no. But I want to be in this world. All the time. I don't want to miss stuff. I'm not choosing to go – do you choose...?

LISA I didn't know anything. I thought it was all normal 'til—

BARRY I wouldn't choose... I want to be with you.

STACY What if you vanish when the baby's born? Can't have you vanishing once the baby's born. That's not a role model. I want a two-parent family. I gotta have – that's what it's about, isn't it? A mum and a dad. I'm not gonna be a sad cow pushing a kid round by myself. That's not what I—

BARRY Course, course.

STACY Feels bad when you're gone.

JACK *(to* LISA*)* Yeah – feels really terrible.

LISA Stop watching that clip.

JACK I was just—

LISA You are – you're just watching it over and over.

JACK Well...

LISA Feels really weird you doing that.

JACK Just want to see if maybe there's some...

LISA Don't. Delete it.

JACK No.

LISA I don't like it. It scares me. Delete it.

JACK It might – it's evidence.

LISA I don't care. It's doing my head in. Give it me. Give it me.

JACK No.

LISA I want it. Don't want you looking at that over and over. Fading disappearing nothing. Fading disappearing nothing. Fading...

BARRY She's right.

JACK Alright alright. I'll look, look...

> **JACK** *goes to delete but whooshing, flashing etc.* **LISA** *and* **BARRY** *disappear.*

Oh. No.

STACY Barry! Barry! This is doing my head in.

JACK How many times it's happened to you?

STACY Four, five times since breakfast. This is my sixth.

JACK Does it get any easier?

STACY No. Still hurts. In your gut. Your heart. Whatever. Miss him.

JACK Yeah – me too.

STACY I couldn't ever get used to a vanishing person.

JACK Maybe we'll have to.

STACY I can't.

JACK But if this is, like, the way it's gonna be.

STACY Then I just can't handle the way it's gonna be.

JACK You'll have the kid.

STACY If it's a stayer. Maybe the kid'll be a vanisher too.

JACK 'Spose.

STACY If the dad's a vanisher then maybe the kid's a vanisher too.

JACK You still want it?

STACY Yeah, only...

JACK You'll cope whatever, won't you? Vanisher or stayer?

STACY I suppose, I don't – this is so new. Vanishers. Stayers. I didn't know there was a difference when I woke up this morning.

JACK Terrible, innit?

STACY Yeah. Terrible.

JACK This could be the rest of our lives.

STACY No.

> **BARRY** *and* **LISA** *reappear.*

Back again.

BARRY Did we...?

JACK You faded away – you dematerialised. You went somewhere—

LISA Oh god. What do you think we are – aliens?

JACK I don't know.

LISA I don't want to be an alien or a ghost. Hold me.

JACK You go out with someone, you live with someone...

STACY You get pregnant with someone—

JACK And then they turn out to be a vanishing person.

LISA Hold me.

JACK I'm frightened.

LISA We're not aliens or ghosts. Hold me. I think we'd know if we were aliens or ghosts, wouldn't we, Barry?

BARRY I think so.

LISA And we'd let you know so don't – hold me. Hold me. Hold me. I'm totally frightened. I'm totally freaked. So don't just look at me like that, staring. Come and hold me.

JACK I'm sorry. *(He holds her.)*

LISA Please don't say those terrible things about us.

JACK Sorry.

LISA Give me a kiss.

JACK ...I can't. Not yet. Sorry, babe.

LISA Oh. I just can't take this. It's doing my head in. I got a kid on the way. But you won't even kiss me. It's too...

Whooshing, flashing etc – LISA *vanishes.*

JACK Oh my god. This is too much. This is gonna drive me mad. I can feel my mind turning. I'm losing it. Losing it. Agggghhhhh!

STACY Come on. Shhhhh. Shhhhhh. She'll be back.

JACK I suppose.

STACY They always come back. Barry's always come back. Barry's here. Look, Barry's here.

BARRY That's right. I'm here for you, mate, yeah? She's bound to come back. Everyone always comes back.

JACK So far. What's she up to – up there?

STACY Don't know.

JACK She could be up to anything right now.

STACY Well I suppose.

JACK Aliens. Aliens experiment on you, don't they? Oh yeah. I've seen it in documentaries. They abduct you, abduct you up to their spaceship and experiment on you. They could be putting an alien baby inside her. Taking out my baby and...

STACY I don't think Barry's been experimented on, have you?

BARRY No. I'd feel it, wouldn't I? I feel like myself. I feel normal. It's you lot act different when I come back. I don't think there's experiments.

JACK You don't know that. They'd wipe you.

Pause.

She's been gone a bit long, hasn't she?

STACY Not that long.

JACK Was Barry ever this long?

STACY Well I'm not sure...

JACK It was just a few seconds before. Only ever a few...

STACY Yeah.

JACK What if she doesn't come back?

STACY She will.

JACK We don't know that. She could have vanished forever.

Long pause.

Look she's not coming, she's not coming back...she oh my god she's not coming back. I've lost her. I loved her and now I lost her.

STACY Give it a bit more time.

JACK I think we should do something.

BARRY Give it time.

JACK It's alright for you – you're one of them – you're an alien or a ghost or whatever but me and Stace, we're normal—

BARRY I'm normal!

JACK Oh no – you go to the secret places, the secret place of the vanished, you've seen the secret place, you don't come back from there normal. *(to the sky)* Give her back, send her back, send Lisa back to us...come on!

BARRY *vanishes.*

STACY Barry! Barry! Oh god.

JACK I'm sorry, Stace.

STACY This is stressing me so much. I'm only two weeks off my due date, I shouldn't be stressing like this. This can't go on forever. Can't live days like this. What we gonna do?

JACK I dunno – maybe scientists or doctors, maybe they'll sort it.

STACY You reckon?

JACK Or the government.

STACY Yeah right.

JACK Or, or, or maybe it's like a – those poltergeist—

STACY Stupid.

JACK There'll be something – it'll be okay. Something'll work out.

STACY I hope so. Not back though, are they?

JACK No.

STACY You really having a baby?

JACK Yeah. Want this. Until I got a kid, I'm a kid.

STACY Same for me... They've not come back.

JACK They will.

STACY Yeah?

JACK They will and then we're gonna stop this.

STACY How we gonna...?

JACK Maybe if we just hold onto them. Hold onto them really tight and don't let them go.

STACY Forever?

JACK Well...

STACY You can't just hold onto someone forever.

JACK We could try. Just 'til the vanishing's over.

STACY Oh.

JACK What?

STACY Something. Baby moving.

JACK Can I listen?

STACY Yeah?

JACK   I'd like to. *(He listens.)* Oh yeah.

STACY   Really – oooo. Better not be – oooo—

JACK   What?

STACY   Contractions. No. I'm alright. Baz has gotta be here if—

JACK   Yeah. I'll look after you if—

STACY   Yeah?

JACK   Make sure you're up the hospital and that you know if you start—

STACY   But you're not the dad.

JACK   No. I know that.

STACY   It's not the same.

JACK   All I'm saying—

STACY   It has to be the dad. It has to be Baz.

JACK   But if he's not here—

STACY   He's got to be here. I need him here. I want him here.

JACK   Yeah but all I'm saying if he's vanished forever.

STACY   He hasn't.

JACK   They're not—

STACY   Nobody vanishes forever. *(clutches stomach)* Ooooo.

JACK   'Nother listen?

STACY   It's not a game.

JACK   Please.

STACY   No.

Doorbell rings. Exit **JACK**, *re-enter with a group of friends [names and genders can be changed here to suit your group]:* **KAREN, HOLLY, TONY, MATT, MARIE, JAMES** – *all talking at the same time.*

KAREN Listen, listen. Something's happening. Something's going on. We've all been vanishing. All of us. We were all round Holly's house and then like Matt vanished first, didn't you—

MATT That's right.

KAREN But then Matt came back again. But then it was Marie, James, me.

TONY. And me,

KAREN One at a time until it was like: who's next? Who's going to go next? Stick together, guys, 'cos we don't know who's going to go next.

HOLLY We are seriously frightened.

Enter **RYAN**, *running after them.*

RYAN It's happening all over the world.

KAREN Yeah?

RYAN Been on the news. Everywhere there's people fading away to nothing. They've got footage from China, America, India – everything. Nobody knows the figures. One in ten. That's what they're saying. One in ten people has already gone but the numbers keep going up – with every minute there's more and more.

JACK They're could be nobody.

KAREN Don't.

JACK By the end of today there could be nobody left.

MARIE Let's pray.

MATT What's that gonna do?

MARIE We gotta do something. *(kneels)* Oh Father who created this world and made everything in it and is now taking away everything in it have pity on us poor children. Spare us spare us spare us.

MARIE *continues to mutter a prayer under.*

STACY I feel so close.

JACK Yeah?

STACY It might happen. What if it happens? I don't want to have my baby like this.

JACK Shhhhhh. Whatever it is – we'll cope.

STACY I want Barry. Barry! Barry! Barry!

JACK Stace – no – you musn't upset yourself – you'll bring it on – Stace!

STACY Barry!

MARIE *vanishes.*

HOLLY Marie. When's it gonna end?

MEGAPHONE *(offstage)* This is the authorities. Stay in your homes. I repeat: stay in your homes.

JACK Oh my god.

MEGAPHONE Anyone leaving their home without authorisation will be shot. We are investigating the vanishings but you must stay in your homes.

Enter **TWO SOLDIERS.**

SOLDIER 1 Whose house is this?

JACK Mine.

SOLDIER 1 The military has taken control. This country is now under military control.

JACK Oh my god.

SOLDIER 1 *(raising gun)* Keep calm.

SOLDIER 2 No harm will come to you if you do exactly as the army say. We are requisitioning a number of houses in which to herd the civilian population – and your house has been selected as a suitable centre for civilians. Do you understand?

JACK I think so.

SOLDIER 1 *(who's been listening on an earpiece)* They're ready to bring in the other civilians.

SOLDIER 2 Good – let's get them in here.

SOLDIER 1 *(calls off)* In here.

SOLDIER 2 Your home is to be the base for the parents and babies group. This way, this way.

> **SOLDIER 3** *marches in a huge range of different parents and babies: single parents and couples, papooses front and back, and buggies, prams – some with twins, triplets. The noise of crying babies fills the air.*

SOLDIER 3 That's it – make room, make room – if you squeeze in – you gotta make room.

SOLDIER 1 *(pointing gun)* Calm and orderly – that's it.

SOLDIER 2 Room for everyone.

> *Finally everyone is in – but it's a very tight squeeze.*

SOLDIER 1 *(with* **MEGAPHONE***)* Everyone sit down. We have to keep order. We have to keep control. Each parent must take responsibility for controlling their baby. No baby is to crawl or in any way move from their buggy or papoose. It is vital that we keep calm. Let's organise entertainment. Can anyone juggle, dance or offer any skills that might amuse the babies?

> *A* **MAN** *or* **WOMAN** *comes forward.*

WO/MAN Me.

SOLDIER 1 Please entertain the children.

> *The* **WO/MAN** *begins to breakdance or juggle or play the ukelele – or anything else that might entertain a large crowd of parents and babies – but after a while*

whooshing, flashing etc. **LISA** *appears. The crowd gasps.*
Entertainment stops.

JACK Lees?

LISA I got to speak to Jack. Where's Jack?

JACK I'm here. Are you alright, Lees?

LISA No. I'm hurting. Oh! *(She collapses.)*

JACK Come on, love. It's alright.

LISA Who are all these people?

JACK You did another vanishing, Lees.

LISA Yeah?

JACK Lots of people are vanishing. It's happening all over.

LISA Ugh. Hurt.

JACK We were gonna have a quiet night in, weren't we?

LISA It's all gone wrong.

JACK It'll go back to normal – everything always goes back
to normal.

LISA It won't. It's not gonna because...

JACK You'll see, everything'll get sorted. We'll be a family.

LISA I want to come back to you – I do.

JACK You're back now, babe.

LISA I'm trying to break through but I can't. I can't stay this
time. The pull's too strong.

JACK Stay, Lees. Forever. I need you here.

LISA I can't. I have to go. I loved this world. I loved you. That's
all I wanted. But I'm lost to this world. I'm lost to home
and shopping and baby and work and you. All that's gone
now. I have to be in the other world – I have to—

JACK Lees – no – don't do that – see all the babies here, Lees? See 'em?

LISA Yeah. Pulling back to the other world.

Whoosh, flash. **LISA** *vanishes. Panic in the crowd.*

MARIE Oh my god that was so horrible – that was like the most horrible thing I have seen in my life ever.

RYAN Do you think she'll come back?

JACK Maybe gone forever.

SOLDIER 2 Order, order – we must have order.

JACK Lisa? Lisa?! Come back come back.

SOLDIER 2 Steady there.

JACK I love you. I want a baby.

SOLDIER 2 Stop or I shoot – you're spreading panic.

JACK But I have to have her. She's everything I need—

SOLDIER 2 *(raising gun)* I have permission to shoot troublemakers.

JACK Shoot me then, go on. What's the point? That's my future just vanished. Better shoot me now. They've all got babies. You've all got babies. That's what I want.

Give me a baby. Give me a baby. I want Lisa back so we can have our baby and fill up the world again. Don't you look at me like I'm a nutter. Just 'cos you got your babies. Could be me. Should be me with a baby.

Whoosh, flash – a third of the people in the room vanish. Pandemonium. Babies howling, parents offering toys and bottles, cooing.

SOLDIER 1 Everybody calm!

KAREN I don't want to go. I don't want to go. Please don't take me.

RYAN It's the end of the world. The end of everything.

HOLLY This is like the most horrible thing that's happened to me ever.

A young **MOTHER** *steps forward from the crowd and talks directly to* **JACK**.

MOTHER My baby. The pram's empty. Look – an empty pram. My baby was three weeks old. But already her eyes followed me around the room. Baby once. Now – empty pram.

JACK It'll all come right.

MOTHER How you know that?

JACK I don't...

MOTHER There's two languages. You got kids or you haven't got kids. And if you haven't got a kid you don't speak the language. It's a love, it's a something, a—

JACK Yeah – but—

MOTHER Sorry. You're just a kid – you don't understand.

JACK Maybe. But I'll understand – yeah. Very soon I'll understand when Lisa—

MOTHER You'll never get your chance. You missed your chance. This is it. This is the world ending. No more people.

JACK No.

MOTHER You say your goodbyes. Now my kid's gone all I want is I go too – listen to all them babies crying. Soon be gone now.

Whoosh, flash – total darkness.

Here we go. We're fading away. All fading away.

The room empties of people. Silence.

JACK Hello? Hello? Anyone there? Anyone there at all?

JACK *uses a lighter to create a little bit of light.*

Is there anyone left? Or am I the only person left in the world? No please don't do that. I don't want to be the only person left in the world. That's horrible. See I won't know what to do if it's just me 'cos I need people to talk to and to do things with. I don't exist if there's no one else. I'm nobody without other people. What are they all doing in the other world? Is there another world? Come on – take me there – I don't want to be like this forever.

He finds a candle and lights it.

STACY Jack – is that you? Have they all gone?

JACK I don't know.

STACY Hello? Hello? They've all gone.

JACK It's just you and me.

STACY In the world – do you think it's just you and me in the world?

JACK Could be... I don't know.

STACY What are we going to do, Jack?

JACK I don't know, Stace.

STACY Jack—

JACK Yeah?

STACY I'm contracting.

JACK What do you mean?

STACY The baby. My contractions.

JACK Are you sure?

STACY Yeah – oh – oh – yeah – I'm sure.

JACK How long have we got?

STACY Few hours.

JACK Maybe they'll come back. Maybe all the doctors and nurses and midwives and everything'll be back in time.

STACY Maybe.

JACK Yeah – we just gotta be brave, we just gotta stick it out and—

STACY Oh oh oh oh oh. It's the stress – brought it on. Oh.

JACK What we gonna do?

STACY I don't – oh oh oh oh oh. What if they don't come back?

JACK They will. They've got too.

STACY How do you know that?

JACK I just...believe.

STACY But it could be you and me and that's it. We could be the human race.

JACK No, no.

STACY Oh. Bigger contractions.

JACK Can't you control it?

STACY No – I can't. I wish I could. But I can't.

JACK *(to sky)* Please – come back. All of you – come back.

STACY Jack – face it. They're not coming back. They're never coming back.

JACK You're scaring me.

STACY This is the world. You and me. And I'm just about to have – oh – once my waters break that's it, you're gonna have to – you're doctor and midwife and—

JACK Why me?

STACY Because there's no one else.

JACK Right.

STACY So get ready.

JACK Yes. Okay, okay. I can do this. I can.

    JACK *cuddles* STACY.

You...breathe and calm and when you're breathing and calm and—

STACY There'll be mess and pain and everything.

JACK It's okay. I know.

STACY You'll have so much to do.

JACK Both of us.

STACY Hot water and towels – kitchen paper and and and—

JACK When we get to that bit. Breathe.

STACY Yeah.

JACK Stace. Do you think this was how it was meant to be?

STACY No I don't. Do you?

JACK I don't... Maybe.

STACY No – this is not supposed to be. This is not normal. This is...

JACK The last thing in the world?

STACY Yeah.

JACK We're all alone now. Just you and me. Listen to that. Nothing. Babies, traffic. Nothing. I reckon there's no one. Anywhere. Just you and me.

STACY Not for much longer.

JACK No?

STACY New one on the way. Are you ready?

JACK I don't know.

STACY You got to be, Jack. You got no choice.

JACK Yeah. Okay. I'm ready.

Scene Two

The living room. Six months later. JACK *and a baby in a pram.*

JACK *(to baby)* And once upon a time there was a brand-new world. And the world had no people. Until – pop – there were two people. And they were called Jack and Stacy.

And after a year there were three people in the world 'cos along came a baby. And they called that baby Kelly. You're lovely, aren't you, Kelly? Yes you are. Your mum's out there somewhere and your mum'll be back soon. And we'll be back together. Family.

Enter STACY, *with a rucksack on.*

How did you get on?

STACY Yeah. Not bad. How's baby?

JACK Baby's good. Took her feed. Nice sleep.

She opens the rucksack for his inspection of contents.

More beans?

STACY Yeah. Sorry. But – look.

She holds up a packet of nappies.

JACK Brilliant. At last.

STACY Yeah.

STACY *takes out a tin of rice pudding and a tin opener and opens it.*

JACK You gonna eat that cold?

STACY I been hunting all day.

JACK You get attacked by them escaped lions again?

STACY No, it's the dogs though. They gone feral. Started hunting in packs. There's a load of them live up the multi storey car park. You have to watch yourself.

JACK Still no sign of any humans?

STACY No.

JACK I told you.

STACY Got to keep looking.

JACK Six months – if there was anyone else we'd have found them by now.

STACY I suppose.

JACK Come on, Stace, there can't be—

STACY Don't you want people? Don't you want the world?

JACK I don't know.

STACY This can't be just – why would it just be us?

JACK Luck. Fate. I don't know.

STACY A thousand – a thousand thousand – miles – there's someone else.

JACK Just you and me and...baby. Stace – don't you think we should give her a name?

STACY No.

JACK I mean six months – "baby" – it might stunt her development, something.

STACY I know, only...

JACK How long you gonna wait?

STACY I want to choose it with Baz.

JACK He's not coming back.

STACY Don't say that. They're all coming back.

JACK Yeah... You got blood.

STACY It's nothing.

JACK Show me.

> STACY *shows her hand.*

STACY There was a cat and a load of kittens sat on the nappies. We had a fight.

JACK See. Told you. Animals are still breeding.

STACY Spose.

JACK She must have met a tom. We gotta look after that.

STACY It's nothing.

JACK I'll bandage it.

> JACK *exits,* STACY *eats rice pudding,* JACK *re-enters with bandage and TCP etc.*

Here we go.

> JACK *dresses the wound, bandages it while:.*

They were noisy – humans – weren't they?

STACY Those elephants down the road make noise.

JACK Just a few of them. They're lonely. But billions of human beings. That was terrible. It's good that they went.

STACY Don't you miss Lisa?

JACK Sometimes.

STACY I thought you were having a kid.

JACK Yeah well she's gone now.

STACY For the moment.

JACK Six months.

STACY But if you're having a kid—

JACK After six months, you move on.

STACY Move on? There's nobody to... The world's empty.

JACK Stace – I get lonely in my bed.

STACY Can't help that.

JACK Sleep with me, Stace.

STACY No.

JACK We don't have to do nothing – just share the bed.

STACY It'll lead to stuff.

JACK It won't. Last two humans – at least we could share the bed.

STACY Forget it. It's not gonna happen. Ugh! She needs her nappy changing.

JACK I'll do it. *(to baby)* Come on, Kelly, we're going to—

STACY What did you call her?

JACK Nothing.

STACY You called her something. Kelly.

JACK Just 'til she gets a real name. It's not good for her.

STACY Oh no, oh no – that is not Kelly, right? That is baby. And I'm not having you doing anything different. Understand? Understand? Give me baby.

JACK I'm gonna—

STACY Give me – now.

> STACY *and baby exit.* JACK *opens a box of cornflakes from the rucksack, starts eating with his hands. Whoosh, flash.* BARRY *appears.*

BARRY Stace? Stace?

JACK Baz? No.

BARRY Stace.

JACK Baz, she's—

BARRY Stace.

Whoosh, flash, **BARRY** *disappears,* **STACY** *re-enters with baby.*

STACY Where's them fresh nappies?

JACK Stace – let's go somewhere. Now.

STACY What do you mean?

JACK The whole world's empty. We could live anywhere. Buckingham Palace. Yeah – let's move. Find somewhere else.

STACY We're fine here. She's used to it.

JACK No – we got to move now. I'll get some things.

STACY Don't be mad.

JACK Make a head start before it gets dark.

STACY I'm not going anywhere.

JACK But it's dangerous here. It's not safe here, please, Stace.

STACY You go.

JACK Please, Stace, you don't understand—

STACY Go.

JACK By myself?

STACY I'm not stupid, Jack. I know what you're up to.

JACK Don't know what you mean.

STACY Playing families.

JACK No.

STACY Well you're not dad, see?

JACK I know but—

STACY So keep away from her. She's my baby. Me. Baz.

JACK Alright – you look after by yourself from now on. I'll hunt for my own food.

STACY You do that.

JACK I will.

STACY My baby. You keep off her, Jack. Piss off – piss off you –
piss off and leave me and my baby in peace.

JACK *reaches into the rucksack and pulls out a
breadknife.*

JACK Right – I gave you a warning. This is what we're doing.
I'm taking charge. We're moving on. Pack a few things and
get down here in ten minutes and we move on or I cut you—

STACY Go on then. Cut me. I don't care.

JACK I will.

JACK *grabs her by the wrists.*

Where do you want cutting first?

STACY Jack, don't.

JACK This is a perfect world. Not having that ruined. You're
not spoiling it for me, Stace. You get born – you think the
world's your mum your dad your brothers sisters. That's
nice. Then you go to school. You got your mates. And that's
good. The world's getting better and getting bigger. Then you
go holiday – see all these other places. Bigger and bigger.
Then you get on the net and you start chatting and you got
friends all over the world. You ever used to do that in the
old days, Stace – before the vanishing – chat to people all
over the world?

STACY Course. Get off.

JACK And I thought that was great. Chatting all over the world.
But then they go – they vanish, they start to fade away and
there's just you and me and me and Kelly.

STACY She's not called—

JACK She's called Kelly, *(waves knife)* alright?

STACY No, I don't wanna—

JACK *slices across her cheek.*

Oooooooo!

JACK Kelly. I name our child Kelly. Kelly – tonight from this moment on, now and forever more you are christened Kelly. No godparents. But – what can you...? Kelly. Kelly. *(to* STACY, *wielding knife)* Yes? Yes? Yes?

STACY Yes. Kelly.

JACK That's it, Mummy. Say, hello Kelly.

STACY ...Hello Kelly.

JACK Tonight, Kelly – Mummy and Daddy are going to have a lovely meal of all the food that Mummy got up the shops then when Mummy and Daddy are feeling nice and tired they are going to go to a big house somewhere a long way away somewhere like Buckingham Palace with a big double bed—

STACY No.

JACK Big double bed and they're going to take their clothes off and they're going to get into the big double bed. And they'll hold each other all night. Mummy's been too shy since you were born to sleep with Daddy but tonight she's not going to be shy. Tonight she'll get over that and she'll hold Daddy. And maybe if the mood's right they'll have sex. Yeah – maybe if it's an extra special night they'll have sex. Yeah. They'll have sex.

STACY I'm not gonna do that.

JACK You'll do just what Daddy tells you to do or I'll – because this is all for Kelly, this is all. We got to be normal. Normal family. In a normal family – baby's got a name, Mummy and Daddy love each other, Mummy and Daddy have sex, Mummy and Daddy try for another baby.

STACY No.

JACK Kelly all on her own. Not good. Not right. So we start working on a little brother or little sister for Kelly. We start working on that tonight.

STACY It's not gonna happen.

JACK It's the normal thing.

STACY Then I'm not going to be normal.

JACK You are.

He slices at her cheek.

STACY Don't, Jack – no. Is there blood?

JACK A bit.

STACY I'll go septic and die.

JACK No.

STACY Yeah. I'll go septic and die and then what you gonna do?

JACK I'm here for you. I'm here to look after us all. I'm gonna mend this and then you're gonna pack our stuff and we're gonna move on to our new place. Go and pack.

STACY I'm gonna change baby. Kelly. Don't hurt her. You can hurt me, only...

JACK I'd never do that. She's everything to me.

STACY Alright as long as...

JACK I know what's best. I'm dad.

STACY Yeah.

STACY *exits with Kelly. Whoosh, flash.* BARRY *appears.*

BARRY Where's Stace...?

JACK Still...a long way away...hunting.

BARRY My kid. Want to see my kid.

JACK Listen, Baz. I gotta tell you...

BARRY Yeah?

JACK World's gone bad. Streets are full of wild animals. Baz, it's really bad here, you don't wanna, the world's such a bad place. Baz...

BARRY Yeah?

JACK And... it's been six months. World moves on.

BARRY Well...yeah.

JACK There's no one left in the world, Baz – 'cept me and Stace and Kelly. Oh yeah. We called the kid Kelly.

BARRY But I wanted to—

JACK Sorry, mate. I delivered the baby. Pain like you wouldn't believe for hours. Stace screaming in your face. I found the baby – guided it down. First pair of hands to guide it. Cut the chord. Cleaned them up – mother and kid. I chose the name. I like it. See and now...we got a bond. Stacy. She's mine.

BARRY No.

JACK And Kelly – we decided it was best, too confusing see. Not gonna tell her about the world before, the vanished people. Decided to tell Kelly I'm her dad. Mummy Daddy and baby.

BARRY You bastard.

JACK Maybe. But that's the way things are. So the rest of you can stay up there or down there or out there or whatever because we don't want you. You're not wanted here. So you stay right where you—

BARRY No!

> **BARRY** *punches* **JACK** *in the stomach.* **JACK** *collapses.*
> **BARRY** *kicks him.*

My kid. My world.

JACK Don't want you. Stay in your world 'cos this world's better without you. I'm King here.

Whooshing, flashing, **BARRY** *vanishes.* **JACK** *is winded.*
Gets up.

Alright, alright, everything's okay. Over now.

Enter **STACY** *with a shopping trolley fully loaded with*
bags etc, wearing a coat.

STACY Did what you said.

JACK Good girl.

STACY Think it's best, innit? If I do what you say?

JACK I don't like forcing you.

STACY Funny way of...

JACK Only sometimes I just see. What's best. For the family.

STACY Right.

JACK You'll like Buckingham Palace.

STACY I'll do what you say.

JACK Stace – you gotta love me.

STACY That an order?

JACK That should come natural.

STACY Well – it's not natural.

JACK Give it time.

STACY No. Anything you want you'll have to use that [*knife*].

JACK If I have to.

STACY Yeah you have to.

JACK Princess Kelly's gonna have her own apartments when
she's older. Her own wing. Kensington Palace.

STACY Let her choose.

JACK She'll need guiding.

STACY Oh. Like we all do – yeah?

JACK Wagons roll.

> **JACK** *puts baby in the pram, starts to push it.*

Come on, Kelly. New home. New start.

STACY Oh I— *(STACY staggers.)*

JACK What?

STACY I – I – I— *(She collapses.)*

JACK Gotta move. Gotta move on. Come on. Gotta get up. Come on.

STACY Jack – I'm – oh!

> *Flashing. Brief vision of the hordes of the vanished. Whooshing. Dies down.* **STACY** *has vanished. Just* **JACK** *and the baby left.*

JACK Right. Right.

> *Pause.*

(to baby) Just you and me. Which is...this is...

> *Pause.*

Once there was a new world. And there was just me in it. And I was all alone. And I grew up. And then one day this baby – pop. I called her Kelly. I looked after her. I fought off the animals. I hunted. I had meaning. I was a King and there was a Princess.

That's good, isn't it? We're the first and one day there'll be – pop pop – from nowhere more babies but until then...

Yeah. You and me. Empty world.

Right. We'll... sleep here tonight. We'll move on in the morning.

Night, Kelly. *(leans into pram, kisses baby)* Night.

And we all slept sound 'cos we were the only two in the world and there was no fighting.

JACK *lies down to sleep, closes his eyes. Flashing, whooshing.* JACK *leaps up.*

Kelly!

Brief vision of STACY *and* BARRY *carrying away the baby. Whooshing, flashing dies down.* JACK *is alone.*

...Empty pram. Empty world.

Long pause.

I was born into this place of the animals and of the shops and the food and the houses.

And I was the only person. The first and the last.

And so I never thought about it. How could I ever think...? If you never knew there were others then...

But sometimes I dreamt, I imagined there were others. Somewhere – others.

Something in this... [*pram*]

But that was fantasy. Because the world is just me. Now and forever. And on and on and good good good.

Only ever me.

So why the— [*pram*]?

A thing from long ago.

Beats the pram rhythmically.

Don't need you. Never need you. Don't know what you're for. You're for nothing.

Nothing. Nothing. Nothing.

You are...a dead thing.

Kicks over the pram, carries on kicking it.

You are a totally dead thing.

I am everything.

I am the world.

So I...

Hunt. Eat. Sleep. Move on. This is my world.

And I...

No if there were never others then there's no loneliness.

No lone...lone...lo...lo...

Lugh. Lugh. Lugh. Lee. Negh. Sssssss.

(ape-like) Ugh ugh ugh.

He's becoming more animal, his centre of gravity moving down.

I ugh oh a oh a ooo m a ugh.

Me.

Me.

Me.

Pattern of movement, almost dancing.

Me.

Me.

Me.

And I.

And I.

And I.

Onto all fours, snuffling and whining. A great animal howl. Then the energy drains from him. Finally, curls up.

Flashing, whooshing. **SOLDIER 1** *appears, brandishing gun.*

SOLDIER 1 Hello? Hello?

> **JACK** *wakes, snarls.*

What the—? What is this place?

> **JACK** *growls, squats, ready to attack.*

Steady. Steady! – I'll shoot.

> **JACK** *bares his teeth.*

Animal.

> **SOLDIER 1** *goes to fire.*

You had your warning.

> **JACK** *leaps at* **SOLDIER 1,** *biting at him and snarling,
> a tussle on the ground. Whooshing, flashing. The room
> begins to fill up with the vanished.* **JACK** *retreats. Soon
> the room is full of the parents and babies, the soldiers,
> the friends and* **BARRY, STACY** *and* **LISA.** *Everyone is
> talking, calling out.* **MOTHER** *with the empty pram steps
> forward.*

MOTHER My kid. My kid. Where's my kid?

> *She disappears into the crowd, searching.*

HOLLY Has it finished? Is it over? Have all those people stopped vanishing?

> **SOLDIER 2** *comes forward, listening on his earpiece.*

SOLDIER 2 *(on* **MEGAPHONE***)* Attention. I have received instructions that it is over. The emergency is now over. The vanished have returned. You are to go back to your homes. There will be a period of transition in which the army will be guiding you. But democracy will return. Back to your homes. Go back home. Normality will be restored. The world is normal again.

JACK *is whimpering on the floor.*

What happened to this one?

SOLDIER 1 Feral. Mad. I can shoot him.

SOLDIER 2 No – leave him there. Alright – come along, everybody – back to your homes.

The room is clearing – **LISA** *comes forward from the crowd.*

LISA Jack, it's me – Lisa. Do you know me – Lisa?

JACK Mmmmgrrrmmmrrr.

LISA Lisa.

JACK I. Me. Duh. Duh. Mad. Mad.

LISA You're not mad, Jack. Look at all the people. Babies.

JACK Uh grrrroooo ooo.

LISA No I wanna human.

STACY *comes forward. She is eight months pregnant.*

STACY You alright, Jack?

JACK Grrrrrrr. Grrrrrrrr.

STACY Jack – what's happened to you?

JACK Grrrrrrrrrrrrrr.

STACY You're frightening.

BARRY Come on, love. Keep away.

STACY Oooo. Felt something. I reckon this baby might come early.

BARRY Shall we pick names?

STACY Tonight? *(to* **LISA***)* Good luck.

BARRY *puts his arm around* **STACY** *and they exit. It's just* **JACK**, **LISA** *and the* **MOTHER** *with the empty pram.*

LISA Come on, Jack. Human words.

MOTHER I got no baby. Pram's empty.

LISA What you gonna do?

MOTHER Search. It hasn't vanished.

LISA Could have.

MOTHER No. I'm a mother. I've gotta find her.

JACK L – l – l – listen.

> **JACK** *stands upright, human.*

> Th – th – th – There's...yeah... There's a place where people go to. They vanish. The people who...yeah.

MOTHER I'll go there and bring her back. I'll carry on.

> *Exit* **MOTHER** *with empty pram. Just* **JACK** *and* **LISA**.

LISA We're all back... Are you human?

JACK Human. Yeah.

LISA Good. I'm hungry. Is there food?

JACK Lees. Where did you go?

LISA Nowhere. Emptiness. It's a blank.

JACK Think. Underworld? Spaceship?

LISA I can't...

JACK Parallel...?

LISA You can ask as many times as you like.

JACK You gotta remember something.

LISA I don't. When you vanish there's nothing.

JACK Maybe you'll get flashes or dreams or...?

LISA Jack. Empty.

JACK It'll come back. One day you'll know what there is.

LISA Maybe.

JACK You'll tell me. It's important.

LISA What did you do?

JACK Eh?

LISA Six months on the planet. What did you do?

JACK I don't know...

LISA You're the only human being who knows.

JACK I – nothing.

LISA Yeah?

JACK Did what I could to survive. Went out hunting. Did what I could for Stace and the baby. There was a baby. Until now she's...she's regressed. Hasn't had... But there was a baby then. I kept things going. Fought. Protected.

LISA Like an animal?

JACK You have to.

LISA They'll be rebuilding the world now.

JACK No more rhinoceros up the shopping centre.

LISA So you can be a human being, yeah?

JACK Do my best. Do you think it was aliens?

LISA Stop.

JACK Maybe if you tried drawing or...

LISA Just stop.

JACK Hypnosis to—

LISA Stop. Stop. Stop. Listen. You are never going to know. Face it. It's not going to—

JACK The mother of my – everyone's been there. Secret. And I don't know it. It's impossible. Can't live with that.

LISA There's no choice.

JACK I want to see inside their heads, their memories—

LISA No.

JACK Cut 'em open: Where did you go? Where did you go?
Where did you go?

LISA Stop it, Jack – you're horrible.

JACK How am I supposed to spend the rest of my life with you
if you got a secret?

LISA It's not a—

JACK I can't do that.

LISA If you want you can go. Leave. There's the door.

JACK Yeah.

LISA You can pack and leave if that's how you feel.

JACK Maybe.

LISA Run off.

JACK Yeah.

LISA Go on.

JACK Yeah. That's best. If I never know you...

Long pause.

LISA You're still here.

JACK I know.

Long pause.

I know.

Long pause.

Yeah.

Long pause. He touches her stomach.

Yeah.

PROPS

Mobile phone (p5)
Papooses (p17)
Buggies (p17)
Prams (p17)
Ukelele (p17)
Baby toys (p19)
Lighter (p20)
Candle (p21)
Rucksack (p24)
Packet of nappies (p24)
Tin of rice pudding (p24)
Tin opener (p24)
Bandage (p26)
TCP (p26)
Box of Cornflakes (p27)
Breadknife (p29)
Shopping trolley loaded with bags (p33)
Coat (p33)
Gun (p36)

LIGHTING

Whoosing/flashing (p5)
Whoosing/flashing (p9)
Whoosing/flashing (p11)
Whoosing/flashing – total darkness (p20)
Whoosing/flashing (p27)
Whoosing and flashing dies down (p35)

SOUND EFFECTS

Whoosing/flashing (p5)
Whoosing/flashing (p9)
Doorbell rings (p14)
Noise of crying babies fills the air (p17)
Baies howling (p19)
Whoosing/flashing (p5)
Animal howl (p36)

VISIT THE SAMUEL FRENCH BOOKSHOP AT THE ROYAL COURT THEATRE

Browse plays and theatre books, get expert advice and enjoy a coffee

Samuel French Bookshop
Royal Court Theatre
Sloane Square
London
SW1W 8AS
020 7565 5024

Shop from thousands of titles on our website

 samuelfrench.co.uk

 samuelfrenchltd

 samuel french uk